AF375493

Welcome,
May this book inspire you, your children, or students to feel the
loving presence of the Earth. The children of the Andes call the
Earth, *"Pachamama."* When read aloud, I hope this book helps you
hear *Pachamama's* voice as if she were speaking directly to you.
May these pages spark your own practice in connecting with the
Earth and giving back to her in gratitude. All our early ancestors felt
and experienced this deep connection to nature, so people around
the world can relearn this practice as our birthright. We are all
children and keepers of the Earth.

Job 12:7-8
But ask the animals, they will teach you;
ask the birds of the air, and they will tell you.
Or speak to the earth, and it shall tell thee.

Dedication

For my grandchildren and all people who cherish,
honor, or protect the living Earth
R.M.

To my Mom
G.A.

Art Direction by Gloria Arteaga

Book Design by Claudia Rivas

SPEAK, PACHAMAMA, SPEAK

Written by **Rebecca Myers**
Illustrated by **Gloria Arteaga**

I am the Earth. I am Pachamama. I am alive!
I am both ancient and ever young. I am as old as
the mountains and as young as the sprouting seeds.
Everything is alive with energy—not only people and
animals, but plants and stones, too.

Like a good mother, I give you everything you need to live—water, food, clothing, shelter, and plants that make air to breathe. I take good care of you.

I give you Beauty everywhere.

Look. You can see me close up in a flower,
a fluffy dandelion, or a field of fireflies.

Look again. You can see me far away in a sunset,
a soaring hawk, or the stars.
What Beauty did you see today?

Listen. You can hear me whenever a bird sings, a best friend laughs, or big trees whisper in the wind. *What Beauty did you hear today?*

Touch. You can feel me whenever you skip a stone,
splash in the ocean, or swish angels in the snow.
What Beauty did you feel today?

Smell. You can smell me whenever you dig in your garden, dance in the rain, or decorate your hair with flowers.
What Beauty did you smell today?

Taste. You can taste me whenever you chug water, chomp into an apple, or chew your dinner.
What Beauty did you taste today?

I am the Earth. I am Pachamama. I am alive!
Bring my Beauty inside you where you can feel it.
Breathe Beauty deep into your heart.

Beauty can feel like gratitude when you're thankful for something. Beauty can feel like kindness. Beauty can feel like love. *Can you feel the Beauty inside you?*

When you feel happy, play outside. Did a squirrel watch you? A bird talk to you? A tree wave hello? *What else did you see?*

When you feel sad, hold a stone, sit against a tree, or walk barefoot on the grass. I can help turn your tears into flowers in your heart.

Put your hand on your heart. *Do you feel it beating?* Lie down on the earth and feel our hearts beating together. Around the world, people drum to the sound of our hearts.

Play with me! I love your songs, your dances, and your blessings. Thank you for remembering I am alive. *What are you thankful for today?*

Take care of me! I love when people think of gentle, kind ways to help me. Please take care of me as I take care of you. *How would you like to help me?*

COMMUNITY GARDEN
Kale
lettuce
Beets
Plant
Trees

I am the Earth. I am Pachamama.
Remember—I am alive!